YOU Could Be a Better Son

7 Steps to Having a Better Son/Father Relationship God's Way

"There is nothing better than spending time with my father"

– Z. Harper

By Zion Harper
Son's Edition

By Zion Caleb Harper

Copyright © 2017 The Awakened Company.

All Rights Reserved. No part of this book or any of its contents may be reproduced, stored in a retrieval system, or transmitted in any form or by any means, electronic, mechanical, recording or otherwise, without the prior written permission of the author.

Printed in the United States of America.

Scripture quotations marked (NIV) are taken from THE HOLY BIBLE, NEW INTERNATIONAL VERSION®, NIV® Copyright © 1973, 1978, 1984, 2011 by Biblica, Inc.® Used by permission. All rights reserved worldwide.

Scripture quotations marked (KJV) are taken from the King James Version. Public domain. http://www.BibleGateway.com.

Scripture quotations marked (NASB) are taken from the NEW AMERICAN STANDARD BIBLE®, Copyright © 1960, 1962, 1963, 1968, 1971, 1972, 1973, 1975, 1977, 1995 by The Lockman Foundation. Used by permission.

Scripture quotations marked (NKJV) are taken from the New King James Version®. Copyright © 1982 by Thomas Nelson. Used by permission. All rights reserved.

The author is providing this book and its contents on an "as is" basis and makes no representations or warranties of any kind with respect to this book or its contents. The author disclaims all such representations and warranties for a particular purpose.

The author will not be liable for damages arising out of or in connection with the use of this book. Using the information contained within, you agree not to hold the author liable for any loss or injury caused by acting on such material or suggestions contained herein.

Editing by www.ChristianEditingServices.com.

Styling by A.J. the Barber of Headquarters Barbershop, Houston, Texas.

Photography by Al Torres Photography, Houston, Texas.

Printing by Disk.com

I would like to dedicate this book to my father for being an awesome parent. He loves, cares for, and protects me. My dad sets an example for me as a Christian and as a young man. Love you, Dad!

Your son,
Zion

Contents

Foreword   7

Preface   9

Acknowledgments   11

1. Listen to the Lesson   13

2. Moments Together: Make Them Count   17

3. I'm Not Perfect, Dad   21

4. Dad, I'm Growing Up!   25

5. He's Doing It for Your Own Good   29

6. My Best Coach Ever!   33

7. The Perfect Son   37

Foreword

It has been my honor to live my life protecting, serving, and raising my son, Zion Caleb Harper. When I think of legacy, I think of Zion and I spending countless hours together, laughing and thinking about what to write and how it would affect fathers and sons today. It is my privilege to present my son to the world as he becomes an independent author at the age of twelve.

Zion knew and accepted God at a young age. The first book he ever read, believe it or not, was the Bible. He has always been thoughtful, caring, and wise beyond his years. Zion is currently an honor roll student in Houston. He loves anything that has to do with basketball and is an awesome athlete.

Zion's purpose for writing his portion of the book was to give encouragement for sons from a son's perspective. Zion has countered every chapter in *You Could Be a Better Father* with advice for every son. He desires that this book inspire sons through hard times; he wants them to get saved, pray to God that things get better, and trust God. Zion also prays that sons do each Buddy Builder exercise to help build a better relationship with their dads.

Sons, enjoy this book, and apply all the chapters to your life. I challenge you and your dad to complete all Buddy Builders in the next six months and watch how God allows you and your dad to have a blast. This book is a must have for all sons who want to be the best son they can.

PASTOR HANSEN ANTHONY HARPER
FOUNDER AND CEO,
KINGDOM IN ACTION OUTREACH MINISTRIES

Preface

Does your dad over-criticize you? Does your dad spend time at home without spending a lot of time with you? Does your dad try to run every little thing you do? Do you and your dad get into arguments over things you say and wear? This book is designed to fix father-son relationships through seven key principles I think will help you to be a better son. I really want you and your dad or father figure to get together and get the meat out of what I'm trying to convey through this book. I want you to know that you guys can have a good father-son relationship if you are willing to listen to God and work together! Thank you for picking up a tool that will change your relationship with your dad forever. Have fun!

Acknowledgments

I would like to acknowledge my mother, Dionne Harper, for giving me ideas for this book. I want thank my dad, Hansen Harper, for guiding me through this journey of writing my first book. I also want to thank my little sister, Zoe, for being an inspiration and sometimes an irritation. Special acknowledgment to my grandparents, Floyd and Ovellia Harper, Ruby Douglas, Reverend Sam Douglas, and Mary Douglas; my uncle and aunt, Reverend Craig Barnett and Donna Barnett; and to all the other family and friends who have supported me through the years.

ZION C. HARPER

1

Listen to the Lesson

Ephesians 6:1–3: "Children, obey your parents in the Lord, for this is right. 'Honor your father and mother'—which is the first commandment with a promise—so that it may go well with you and that you may enjoy long life on the earth" (NIV).

Hello. I'm Zion Harper, and I'm eleven years old. You know, last year, I didn't have good listening skills. When I was at basketball practice in my local basketball league and somebody like my coach told me to do something, either I would not be paying attention or I would say, "Yes, sir" and not do what was commanded. Sometimes my coach and my dad both had to yell and get onto me to make sure I was listening to them and paying attention.

All the yelling and getting on my case for things paid off. Over time, I became a great listener and a great player. It's the same way with your dad. When your dad tells you to do something, you really want to do it. When he tells you, he will sometimes yell, but your dad is trying to tell you something important. You might wonder why your dad is telling you these things and why he is yelling and screaming, because I feel like that with my dad sometimes too.

For example, sometimes I like to tuck my shirt into my pants to feel comfortable and natural. I know it isn't natural at all, but I thought it was a good way to look. We were going to Vacation Bible School last summer, and my dad saw my Buckee T-shirt tucked in. So he said, "Why is your shirt tucked into your pants?"

I said, "I have it tucked in because my shirt feels very big!"

After that my dad said, "Untuck your shirt, because that makes you look cool and regular."

I was saying in my head, "Why do I have to do this? Why do I have to untuck my shirt?" During this time, the other side of my head said, "Just untuck your shirt. Dad knows what he's doing."

So we went into the church, and my dad and mom registered me, and everything ended up going well. Nobody said anything about my shirt being too big or anything like that. Now, what if I'd gone my own way and kept my shirt tucked in? Somebody probably would have said, "Why is your shirt tucked in? That looks really bad!"

My experience shows that, besides God and the Holy Spirit, your dad is the wisest dad out there, and you should listen to him no matter what. Your dad has been on the earth way longer than you, so he knows what goes on and how to handle things. So it's important to listen to your dad no matter what.

Now, what if you were in the NBA and were selected by the Cleveland Cavaliers in the NBA draft, and you didn't really know what to do? Would you have Lebron James as your mentor and listen to him? Or would you go your own way and do what you think is right? Common sense would be to follow Lebron James. He's a two-time champion and four-time MVP. Lebron is one of the best players ever to play in the league.

It's the same thing with your father. It's common sense to listen to your dad. He is older, wiser, and smarter than you are. Even though it's sometimes tough to listen, listen to him anyway, and learn the lesson your dad has been showing you.

Lessons I Learned

- Our dads have very good advice if we just take the time to listen to them.

- You should listen to your dad no matter what.

Buddy Builder

Go grab your dad and pray with him. When you pray, pray that God would give you the ability to do what your father says joyfully.

Moments Together: Make Them Count

Ecclesiastes 3:12–13: "I know there is no good in them, but for a man to rejoice, and do good in his life. And also that every man should eat and drink, and enjoy the good of all his labor, it is the gift of God!" (KJV)

The time you spend with your dad is precious. When you spend time with your dad, you have to make something fun out of it. Even the smallest things can be made into special memories. I remember that one day when I was four, Dad decided to have a barbeque and play on the Slip 'N Slide. After we ate and settled our food, my dad and I got on it. We had loads of fun until it got dark outside. When we came back into the house, we were exhausted but happy. That's one memory I'll never forget.

When you make something fun out of something little, it can and will be a special memory. Sometimes special memories can come out of nowhere too. Last September, my great-grandfather passed away, and my dad was very sad about it. We were in school at the time, and my mom and dad are teachers. My dad wanted to go, but he knew it would cost a lot of money to travel from our home in Houston to Gary, Indiana, where his family lives, for the funeral. My dad was just thinking about sending flowers up to pay his respects, but then he decided to drive to the funeral after all and take me with him. I was thinking at the time that it would be a just okay trip. However, even though we were on a strict budget on food and gas, we had a great time. My dad and I talked and laughed and bonded with each other all the way to Indiana. On the way to the funeral, my dad let me know that my aunt wanted me to say a speech at the funeral. I decided to do a speech called "Strength." After I read it at the funeral, the whole church stood to their feet.

Overall, it was a great trip. Sometimes special times happen even when you don't think it will be good or fun. It's like God comes in like a whirlwind and turns something that should be bad into something incredible. Unexpected memories come from God.

Now, big, special moments should really be cherished, because you can never get those times back. During one Thanksgiving week, my dad took me to a Houston Rockets game against the Los Angeles Clippers. We had so much fun! We ate well, we saw the Rockets play hard, and at halftime we went to the play area in the upper deck where they had a whole lot of other stuff for kids to do. Even though the Rockets lost in a great battle, we had a great time. My dad and I really bonded.

Special memories with your father come at all different times and in all different sizes. But it's how you cherish your memories that determines whether they're special or not. When you have moments together with your father, make them count! When you're with your dad, try to leave your phone behind. If you don't, you won't be paying full attention to your dad, and you might miss out.

Lessons I Learned

- The time you spend with your dad is precious.

- Make sure you're focused and attentive when you spend time with your dad. (Put all electronics away.)

Buddy Builder

Do a project with your father. You can go to Hobby Lobby, Walmart, or Home Depot and find all types of materials and kits to have a blast with each other. You can also search on YouTube to learn how to make these projects.

3

I'm Not Perfect, Dad!

Romans 3:23: "For all have sinned and fall short of the glory of God." (KJV)

We're humans, and we aren't perfect. We all make mistakes once in a while. Sometimes our dads will expect us to be perfect in all we do, especially in sports. If you're doing your best at whatever you do and giving it your all but your dad keeps getting on you for not doing something, you have to be respectful and say, "I'm not perfect, Dad. Could you please stop getting on me for every little thing?" If you do that and say it kindly and respectfully, he will more than likely stop.

For example, a few months ago, my AAU basketball team qualified for a tournament in Dallas. My dad's cousin Kelsey lives in Dallas, so he came to my game. After the game my dad was talking to my coach and some other people about how I need to get better. Kelsey was also telling me what felt like hundreds of things I needed to do differently on the basketball court. So I was feeling as if my father and everyone else were against me. Kelsey is over fifty years old, and he was trying to show me how to be tough, so he came up to me and pushed me. I pushed him back, but I fell to the ground and broke down crying.

After I got up and my cousin and I made up and hugged, my dad and I got into the car and rode back to the hotel. On the way, I kindly and respectfully told my dad, "I'm not perfect, Dad. Could you please stop getting on me for every little thing?" After that, my dad calmed down with all the talk about how I needed to get better and all that other stuff. He told me, "Let's just relax for the rest of the night."

It's like at the end of the movie *The Karate Kid*, when Jaden Smith rose up with one foot and had his head sideways. When he was calm, the other guy was calm too. When you're calm and you speak what's on your mind respectfully toward your father, he will peacefully react to what you say.

Hey, you aren't perfect! We all aren't perfect! Even though we aren't perfect, we must give everything our best effort. When we do that, our dads will be proud of us, and they'll listen to what we have to say.

When your dad gives you correction, sometimes you have to listen to his *words* more than you listen to his *tone* of voice. Then you can come back later when everything is calmer and talk to him respectfully about what happened and how his tone made you feel. But don't miss out on good advice because it was delivered the wrong way.

Lessons I Learned

- Your dad is not perfect, and neither are you.
- Respectfully and calmly tell your dad what is on your mind, and usually your father will respond calmly.

Buddy Builder

It's acting time, guys. Sons, go to your dads and act out these two examples of a conversation between a son and his dad. Be ready to explain how the conversation between both could have been better.

Father: Jason, didn't I tell you to have all your clothes on for school? Why do I have to tell you the same thing over and over again? Stop acting like a four-year-old!

Son: I'm getting to it, Dad. Get off my case!

1. What was the main point the dad was trying to get across to his son? _____
   _____
   _____

   How should the son have responded to the father? _____
   _____
   _____

Father: Jonathan, your room is a mess! You're living like a pig. This is ridiculous! What is wrong with you? Get this room straightened up right now, or I'll give you something to frown about!

Son: You never say anything to Mary about *her* room. You always pick on me. I can't wait to go to Grandma's.

2. What was the main point that the dad was trying to get across to his son? _____
   _____
   _____

   What should the son's response have been?
   _____
   _____
   _____

Dad, I'm Growing Up!

Proverbs 22:6: "Train up a child in the way he should go, and when he is old he will not depart from it" (NKJV).

Hey! You're growing up! You're starting to wear deodorant, or you might be starting to grow hair under your armpits. Some stuff you were interested in when you were little, like dinosaurs or Hot Wheels cars, might not be as interesting to you now.

Your dad might not remember that at certain points. He might even embarrass you without even knowing it. Here are some ways to let your dad know you're growing up:

1. Reason with your father in a nice and respectful way. As I said earlier, if you tell him what is on your mind calmly, you will probably get a calm answer from your dad. For example, one day when I was eight years old, our family

decided to go to Quiznos for lunch. So we got there and my dad said, "Okay! Order off the kids' menu." I ordered off the kids' menu and ended up getting this little itty bitty sandwich with a tiny pile of chips. It was a four-year-old's meal! I gobbled the little baby food up and was still hungry. Then I told Dad that the meal wasn't big enough for me, and I started to cry. (Please try not to cry when you talk to your father. Talk to him calmly instead.) When I asked my dad for a bigger meal, he let me get a bigger meal; no big deal. If you calmly ask your dad for more, he should calmly respond and say *yes*.

2. You might have to laugh at yourself sometimes. I learned this when my dad and I went to one of his former pastors, Mr. Davis. We went to see his wife because she was in the hospital here in Houston. When we went into the room, all of us reunited and talked. After a while, my dad started talking to them about how, when I was little, I used to run around the church. Then suddenly everyone was staring at me. At the moment, I just laughed. I laughed at myself because I knew saying something like "Why are you all staring at me?" wouldn't be worth saying. If I hadn't relaxed, a nice moment would have turned into a horrible

moment. Sometimes things can just be left alone.

3. Be careful when you ask for something bigger. Get ready for that certain responsibility. Sometimes doing what you normally do is the best thing you can do. For example, my dad and I went to wash clothes at the Laundromat one day. I put the quarters into the machine to make it start, and suddenly my dad said, "Zion, now let's see if you can wash clothes by yourself." So I put the detergent into the washer. At the moment I pressed "start," my dad realized I hadn't put the clothes into the machine. Oh, no! I had messed up the washing process. My dad yelled, "Hey—you forgot to put in the other basket of clothes. That's five dollars wasted!" I felt terrible. I learned that sometimes *thinking* you know what to do versus actually *knowing* what to do are two different things. Be satisfied with what you have. Growing up can be good and bad. Maybe your father needs to know that. If at the right time you calmly let your dad know that you want more responsibility, you might get more. If you laugh about yourself sometimes when your dad treats you like a little kid, it will help you release the feeling of getting mad. If you pray to God to be thankful, you will be more grateful and less

greedy. If you do these things at the right time, your dad will know you're growing up.

Lessons I Learned

- Dads know that we're growing up and may tell embarrassing stories about us. We shouldn't take it personally. Instead, we should respond to our dads calmly and laugh it off.

- Our dads will give us more responsibility if we show them they can trust us.

Buddy Builder

Ask your dad to go to the movies and see a movie you want to watch. Have a great time. Get popcorn, candy, Slushies, and any other great snack you both want. Afterward, talk to your father in a respectful tone about three things you don't like or don't want to do anymore.

He's Doing It for Your Own Good

Ephesians 6:1–3: "Children, obey your parents in the Lord, for this is right. 'Honor your father and mother'—which is the first commandment with a promise—so that it may go well with you and that you may enjoy long life on the earth" (NIV).

Why do I have to have my pants a certain way? Why do I have to talk in a specific manner? Why do I have to do things I don't like? Why? Why? Why?

Do these sound like questions you ask your dad? Well, everything has a purpose, and the things your dad is telling you are for your own good. Yes, he might not do something like take you to a fun carnival or to the ice cream parlor. But it might be for a bigger and better reason. Fathers see farther ahead of us and keep us from getting into *big* trouble.

That's why taking to heart Ephesians 6:1–3 is so important. It says, "Children, obey your parents in the Lord, for this is right. 'Honor your father and mother'—which is the first commandment with a promise—so that it may go well with you and that you may enjoy long life on the earth" (NIV). When you obey your father and do what he tells you, you'll do great in everything you do. Obeying your parents will always keep you on the right track.

When I was about six or seven, I was in charge of handling the shopping cart at the grocery store, but I was bad at it. I kept bumping into shelves and people. My father had to keep telling me to watch where I was going. I don't remember crying, but I might have; I was very emotional at that age. My dad pushed the cart for the rest of the time at the store.

Even though I was mad, I had to flash back. I was hitting, bumping, and crashing into everything and everyone in sight. What if my dad just kept letting me use the cart? Maybe I would have bumped into the wrong person who would want to do something bad to me. Our fathers are trying their best to look after us. They try to see ahead of us. Even though you may think your dad is going overboard, he's doing it for your own good.

Lessons I Learned

- Fathers see farther ahead of us and keep us from getting into *big* trouble.

- Though we don't always agree with our dads and might think they are going overboard in their decisions, they're doing everything for our own good!

Buddy Builder

Ask your father to take you both to the barbershop. Take a photo of you and your dad after the haircut. Tell your dad one or two things you like about his haircut. Take the photo and get it developed. Hang the picture on the refrigerator for long-lasting memories!

6

My Best Coach Ever!

Proverbs 13:1: "A wise son heeds his father's instruction, but a mocker does not respond to rebukes" (NIV).

My dad is my best coach ever, not just in sports but also in life. He helps me with everything I should do, and he loves me very much. My dad guides me through lots of things, including sports and academics. My dad is my best coach ever, and your dad is yours also. Dads practically have a playbook in their minds. Fathers do some things that might not appeal to you, but it will assist you for the game of life. For example, if your dad tells to tie your shoes a certain way or to put clothes on in a particular way, you should do it. Do everything your dad says, because he has experienced the game of life. He has experienced things you haven't. Doing what your dad says is important for everything you do.

My dad is the assistant coach on my basketball team. He is more of an encourager on my team. He has always been there at my games to support me. Outside of basketball, too, my dad tells me what I am doing right and what I am doing wrong. He tells me the right plays in the playbook. My dad guides me to executing plans. For example, I remember my little sister, Zoe, coming home from school one day saying that she got slapped in the face. After my dad heard, he had a long pep talk with my sister and me about how we need to defend ourselves. The crazy part is that two days later, I got into a fight myself. I was in P.E. class, we were playing basketball, and this one guy got upset because he was losing and pushed me to the ground. So I kicked him in the knees and punched him in the face. After about a minute of fighting, the gym teacher broke it up. We went to the principal's office, and I called my dad. Dad was proud of me for defending myself. I got a day in detention, but I knew I'd done the right thing. My dad told me to defend myself if someone hit me, and I did exactly that.

My dad also is my best coach spiritually. He always encourages me to read the Bible and pray every day. My dad always wants me to be involved with God. One time when I was about seven or eight, I was ready to watch cartoons. After an hour, my dad woke up and asked me if I had read the Bible. I said no. So he gave me a Psalm to read. He then explained the scripture to me. We prayed, and he told me something very important. He told me to read a Psalm every day according to what day it is. For example, if today was the thirtieth, I would read Psalm 30. After that, my dad read to me Matthew 6:33, "Seek ye first the kingdom of God, and his righteousness; and all these things shall be added unto you" (KJV). That is basically instructing you to do something that relates to God, like reading the Bible or praying, before you start the day.

My dad is my best coach ever. Your dad is yours also. He loves you in everything you do. Since your father is the best coach, do everything he says. When you execute everything he says, you'll always be great!

Lessons I Learned

- Do everything your dad says, because he has experienced the game of life.

- Read your Bible daily and have a discussion with your dad about what you've learned.

Buddy Builder

Sons, go meet up with your dad to complete this Buddy Builder. Play a game or sport you both like.

The Perfect Son

John 8:29: "And the one who sent me is with me, he has not left me alone, for I always do what is pleasing to him" (NRSV).

We always want to be perfect and do everything our fathers say, right? But we aren't perfect. I make mistakes; you make mistakes; we all make mistakes, because we're human.

There is one Son who *is* perfect, however, in everything his Father told him to do. That Son is Jesus Christ! Jesus is the perfect Son. He is the perfect Son because he is the Son of God. God has never sinned, so since Jesus is the Son of a perfect God, he has never sinned either.

Jesus is the perfect Son of God because he was devoted to God's Word. He read and it and took it to heart. Since he was so devoted to his father's commandments, he knew right from wrong and never sinned. For example, Matthew 4:1–11 talks about how Jesus was tempted by Satan to turn rocks into bread. Jesus answered, "It is written: 'Man shall not live on bread alone, but on every word that comes from the mouth of God'" (Matthew 4:4 NIV). Then Satan tried to tempt Jesus to throw himself down from the highest point in the city. The devil told Jesus that God would tell his angels to protect him. Jesus answered, "It is also written: 'Do not put the Lord your God to the test'" (Matthew 4:7 NIV). Finally, the devil took him to a very high mountain and showed Jesus all the kingdoms of the world, and he offered Jesus all of them if he would only bow down to him. Jesus commanded Satan to get away from him and told him that God is the only one to be worshiped and served.

You see, because Jesus was devoted to his Father's commandments, he never sinned. He's the Son of God, and He's perfect. Jesus is the only perfect person who has ever lived.

Jesus is the perfect Son because he obeyed God even though it meant dying. Philippians 2:8 says, "Being found in appearance as a man, He humbled Himself by becoming obedient to the point of death, even death on a cross" (NASB). Now, dying on the cross was one of the most humiliating forms of death in Bible times. People spit on, beat, and slapped Jesus. Jesus didn't have to die for us. He was perfect and obeyed everything God the Father said and never sinned. He obeyed even though no one really helped him or was by his side. Matthew 26:36–46 talks about how Jesus was praying to God that the burden of death for the whole world would be taken away from him.

Before he prayed, he told his disciples to wait and watch with him. Jesus found all his disciples asleep when he returned. Judas even betrayed Jesus. How could he do that after all Jesus had done for him?

But we are just like those disciples. We aren't perfect sons as Jesus was. We slip up, make mistakes, and do wrong. But we should always try to model Jesus by being obedient to our earthly fathers and our heavenly Father. Obedience will always make your earthly father and your heavenly Father pleased. But remember: Jesus is the perfect Son, and nobody but Jesus is perfect. Since he is the perfect Son, all sons should model him!

Lessons I Learned

- As sons, we make a lot of mistakes. But there is no perfect son except for Jesus.

- The life of Jesus is the perfect blueprint of how to be a perfect son. Let's follow Jesus and his example.

Buddy Builder

Son, confess this to your dad:

Dad, I know I'm not a perfect son, but in my heart I desire to be a good son. I want to reassure you that I respect and honor you as my father. I want you to forgive me for doing sonship my way and not God's way. From this day forward, I pledge these seven things by the grace of God:

1. I will learn the lessons you are trying to teach me.

2. I will value every moment we spend together.

3. I will value your opinion in my decision-making, because I know I'm not perfect.

4. I will respectfully ask you to give me space when I need it.

5. I will not be upset when you tell me no, because I know you want only the best for me.

6. I want to assure you daily through my attitude, words, and deeds that you are and always will be my best coach ever.

7. With God's help, I will be devoted and obedient to your leadership as Jesus was obedient to his Father.

Then say this to yourself: *I am the perfect son—through God's grace. Amen!*

Thank you for purchasing Better Father/Better Son

Hansen and Zion Harper are available for seminars, conferences, and key note speaking opportunities.

For more information please go to
www.betterfatherbetterson.com

www.ingramcontent.com/pod-product-compliance
Lightning Source LLC
Chambersburg PA
CBHW061517040426
42450CB00008B/1669